Freud in Brooklyn

Freud in Brooklyn

Joanna Fuhrman

Hanging Loose Press
Brooklyn, New York

Published by Hanging Loose Press, 231 Wyckoff Street, Brooklyn, New York 11217. All Rights Reserved. No part of this book may be reproduced without the publisher's written permission, except for brief quotations in reviews.

Hanging Loose Press thanks the New York State Council on the Arts for a grant in support of the publication of this book.

Printed in the United States of America
10 9 8 7 6 5 4 3 2 1

The cover photograph of Dreamland was taken by the *Brooklyn Daily Eagle* and is now in the Brooklyn Collection of the Brooklyn Public Library.

Cover design by Pamela Flint

Acknowledgments: Some of these poems appeared in the following publications: *6,500, Brooklyn Review On-Line, Cello Entry, Fence, Hanging Loose, Lungfull!, Poetry Northwest, The Oregonian, The Plain Truth of Things,* and *Puerto del Sol.* Special thanks from the author to Linda Bierds, Heather McHugh, Jean-Paul Pecqueur and David Wagoner for their criticism and encouragement. Also thanks to the New York Mills Arts Retreat and the Stadler Center for Poetry at Bucknell University.

Library of Congress Cataloging-in-Publication Data

Fuhrman, Joanna
    Freud in Brooklyn / Joanna Fuhrman
      p. cm.
      ISBN 1-882413-73-3 — ISBN 1-882413-72-5 (pbk.)
      I. Title.
PS3556.U3247 F74 1999
811'.54—dc21   99-058982

Produced at The Print Center, Inc. 225 Varick St., New York, NY 10014, a non-profit facility for literary and arts-related publications. (212) 206-8465

Contents

Personal Ad

For my Mom and Dad

Out of the Picture

Watching Trains

A blue arm stuck out of the train's window
    and a cat-shaped figure wavered, suspended

over the moving ground.

You could see the figure shifting backward as the train went
    forward.

As the train went forward, you could see the figure shifting
    backward

Somehow, you knew what you couldn't know:

that the arm protruding from the window was a man's arm,
not a woman's,

and the cat-shaped figure, hanging in the air, was really a
    cat,
not a cat-shaped toy.

There was no clatter from the tracks,

no sound of cat or man or train.

By your window, you drank cola from a long straw.
Wet hair clung to your scalp.

There was no clatter from the tracks,

no sound of cat or man or train.

A flute's crescendo challenged the radio's static.

The train rushed forward. The cat back.

Freud in Brooklyn

Sigmund Freud is walking out
of the picture. His feet cut off. His face
blurred by the shadow of his fedora's rim.
He looks away toward the Atlantic.
The ocean is just a gray smudge,
the size of an index finger's tip.

Freud traveled to New York mainly
to see Coney Island's Dreamland Park.
He had read about the fake tenements there,
burned down twice a day for Lower East side immigrants
to gawk, and about the newborns in the incubator exhibit,
pink and wrinkled as a vulture's cheek,
their names written on the glass in bubble print.
Freud became obsessed with the Coney Island lion,
"so huge the concrete under him had cracked,"
read the *Tagezeitung*, and with
the thousand glass cranes in the glass house
and with the fantasy ride on Pike's Pier,
the three dimensional panorama of Hell.

In Hell, Freud read, the tourist enters a boat
and descends. He's soon surrounded
by pink glass flames, a Bach toccata
and a tunnel painted with a mural of judgment day,
Jesus standing on a *trompe l'oeil* cloud,
his gold robes weightless in the wind.
Candles light up his eyes.
When the tourist feels he's about to leave,
a trumpet sounds and thirty papier mâché devils fall.

In Vienna, Freud dreams about Coney Island's Hell.
His eyes close and he enters the boat,
feels it seal around him like a skin.
Each devil has the face of a different patient.

First, the wolf man baring his teeth.
Then Anna O. grinning.
Freud says "Come with me in my sleek new boat."
They say very sweetly "no."

At this, he wakes and puts on his slippers
trudges to his terrace.
It's May, the pale azaleas are half
on the branch, half torn
under the wooden wheels of old buggies.
He watches children playing in the street.
A girl with a sash over her eyes spins
until she falls down laughing.

When Freud's ship docks in New York,
Dreamland has already started burning.
Something about the hot tar was off
and set the park on fire.

Heaven's soon ablaze.
The angels' wings melt. God on his throne
with his fake gold scepter explodes in a giant roar,
starting the burning in Hell.
The glass flames turn the fire blue.
The devils vanish as they touch the flame.
Even the wet boats burn,
the water under them black as char.

As Freud checks into his room
on East Fourteenth Street,
much of the park is ash.
The burning inches toward the famous lion
as he paces in his wrought iron Art Nouveau cage.
The tamer stands frozen, watching for awhile,
and then, out of love, he shoots.

Over Cobblestones and Dirt

Rolling their barrel over cobblestones and dirt,
the two men keep walking,
waving to the crowd gathered to gawk.
    In the barrel lie the men's
whole lives: a Sienna photograph
stained by coffee, a bundle
of fish jerky and a dog—
tied to the inside by thick black cords
so that his body rotates
as the barrel rolls.
    By dusk, the smell of burning toffee
and damp leather boots has the men high. They long
to recognize a face in the burgeoning crowd.

Finally, as they reach the outskirts of Berlin,
a woman with a burlap sack full
of potatoes calls out. The men
have never seen her before.
They continue to walk, rolling their barrel
over cobblestones and dirt.
    The dog though, inside the barrel,
lets out a deep red howl.
He bites out of his cords and runs.
He runs and runs
towards the woman waiting
in her almost empty field,
the round sun defining the sky
behind her, her potatoes bulging
like a toddler from her arms.

A Meritorious Act

By the five and dime, us brains hung,
swapping chordates. We were fine flock indeed—
double-jointed in an intellectual sense.

We could never have guessed that the next year
number three would take up snorkeling or that
number seven would defend fascism

on his honeymoon with Lib. It was a brain thing,
as they say, but what made us brains a thing
in the midst of so many, what must be non-things

(e.g. the rushing of caterpillar hairs,
the warmth of a bath)? You know
it was us who stole the silverware

from the dinosaur museum:
number eight in his snowflaked ski-mask,
number two schlepping her ex's binoculars,

number eleven dangling like an extra
light bulb from the pterodactyl chandelier.

Advice for Absent-Minded Detectives

Always when we discover the lying machine,
it is August and sun illuminates the feathers

in a mud-made nest. Counting backwards,
we uncover the cracked armor of an absent snail,

twin twigs and a boulder with its sediment shifting.
Later we'll find: a doll's ear glued to a cheek,

a mouth painted on a drugstore window.
Some will question why the monocle

was water-dipped or why the rabbit
acquiesced to the children's pawing fists.

So let me clarify: it's not the clues,
but the pre-clues, we are after,

(not the questions, but the waves before the words)

not the footsteps leading to the library safe,
but the path emerging before the falling feet.

Thirty and Still Too Cool

"If you were a poem, I would not be its writer."
                                    —Bill Knott

Her glare could freeze a neighbor's sweat. Could slice
through heat like an X-ray examining luggage.

Beware: words are portioned. Count yours before
the clock stops and the smell of bourbon breaks

its old eggs open. If she lowers her voice,
pump up the radio's volume. If she stands,

let the chair under her crumble.
Too cool to wait for the sun to lift out

of the sky, she waves her hands
in flames. Nobody's watching.

Germ Land: The Theatrical Debut

A burlap sack rigid from shellac
makes a perfect hat. Wearing it,
I step before the mass
of youthful eyes. For the hour,
I'm Newmonia, war correspondent
for the White Plague Promoter,
and a belter of spiffy tunes.
Teddy the Tubercle, wrapped
in shinlike red and membraned white,
he's my dancing partner,
all swift kicks and low notes.
For once, I'm not part of the chorus,
just another influenza or bacillus.
Who needs another flying foot,
another cell in line!

Atlantis

After the gods left, the trucks of evening
arrived. They were slow as a filmed sunset
but we loved them anyway. We smelled
their heat through our chlorine soaked skin.

After the gods left, we took up digging.
Bought goggles to wear

when the sun turned red. We watched
the final airport close. So brave a tune
we played that night, fiddles burst into wings.
Grass refused to grow.

I thought a new city might rise:
built from our tunes. Instead, a sameness fell.
Gods left. Trucks stayed.

Piazza

A four-star accountant wrestles
a three-star singer on the *Piazza
of our Dear* while a two-star
chaplain shoots pictures
with an eight-star camera.
"Look!" his friend insists, pointing
to a thin-wristed three-star ingenue.

Everyone here is always waiting:
the three-star dog barking
some national anthem, the half-star
kid dragging a cut balloon
string, the four-star chef
watching his ice sculpture melt.

Everything here is always
waiting. Every potential
painting has been composed
and recomposed, noses
reshaped by women in white,
eyes lit by lights,
hands stretched by cats.
With an official broom, a once
lover clears an antenna away.
With an official wink, a once friend
wiggles her special occasion teeth.

The Now

A house moves through space on stilts.
Windows darken. The smell
of smoked tomatoes drifts in
from the cellar. You push everything aside,
the long silver needles with which you knit,
your flaming red purse, the radio's hiss,

and you walk through a window.

Here, the letter you wrote yesterday
rewrites itself. A Siamese cat dangles
from a macramé plant hanger. An old man,
bare muscles gleaming in the dim red light,
lays bricks on a two-foot mound.

Skylight

If the brain is just a final organ,
who cares if the ego-catcher sorts
flies or if the letter opener is moist
from licked fingers? A skylight's
just enough to define a neck jutting
from a chest, or to reveal
the curve of a lip-shaped light.

The secrets are still here. Stop
that chomping on the brittle bar!
The devouring plots I meant
to leave under the paisley
scarfed light, they're here too.

It's not the ghost of thin french fries
or the inner workings of a dentist's clock
that lures us back. No, no
it's that damn red dot,
announcing its presence
erasing our predictable retreat.

Evidence

If you don't blink, nothing is funny or so
a scientist says, as he measures the wingspan
of an extinct Arctic hummingbird.

Similarly if you hear a sad story eating peanut butter
you will not cry out. This test has been replicated underwater
and out of Earth's atmosphere. Nobody ever cries out.

Once a girl in Tuscaloosa wrote an evolution of beetles
in green ink. When she went swimming
a new story sprang up. She felt a loss like birth.

Reporters swarmed, snapped her picture
for cereal boxes. Asking, "could she blink?
Had she tried eating peanut butter in bliss

or mixed with honey in a submarine."
The girl laughed. With her plastic flower,
she shot the reporters wet

and left. Some speculate there were confounding factors
to her flight: the smell of southern wheat or
the warm touch of sun off apricot dashboards.

No one can quite grasp the cause.

O but what we can imagine:
the reporters and their subjects and us,
drinking iced tea under trees' lush canopies,
pollen flush from cut kudzu.

All evidence drifting away—

"In a Little Box"

Even in death,
he figured, an emperor
should win out.
Reasonable men
might have objected
to the skin's fresh hue,
the vinyl shininess etc.,
the touched-up lips.

Instead, they changed the phrase
he coined. "In a little box"
became "in a little hole"
became "what he hid away,"
became "what he meant,
but made a decision not to say."

Another Hypothetical Question Ignored

As a toddler pushes her stroller past
the rhododendron's pornographic
buds, a broken underground sprinkler shrieks,
a man tying a kayak to a car

clears his throat. White petal flakes fall.
A starling descends, sidewalk to road,
and an old woman stands, straddles
her purple Schwinn, pivots

her head and listens through
a window to the voice
of a teenage tenor, rattling glass.

Geese

I

His nurse stands on the dock,
the tops of her feet sunburned from waiting.
In the distance, the Center's glass cafeteria,
the rows of well-pruned shrubs.

As he floats on the lake, she can see him
in her mind,
drifting to shore.

She knows he will hold
each grain of rice
in his hand before he puts
it in his mouth.
For him, the first
is a goddess's eyelash,
the second, a thin slice of sky.

II

The sun has already hidden behind the gray tree's head.
The patient has not come back
as expected. He drifts
watching the leaves
from the sassafras tree
fall and float
as one by one
the migrating geese
land on the lake's skin.

She knows she should call
for help, to get him off
the lake before dark.
Instead, she waits,
calls to him,
repeating his name.

No reply

except for a song
she imagines he is singing:

she listens for it

in the light
over the high cries of geese

the falling and rising,
the rising and the fall.

Before Words

Past the abandoned lobster stand with its high red tent flap-
    ping,
over nothing but a rusted table and a sign OBSTER HERE,
past the girl in her gingham print dress with her giant red
    binoculars,
past the dog sniffing the brine-colored remains of a codfish,
past the sparrow hovering confused by an oxidized bronze
    pelican
on a half eroded post, the foam expands: elastic, volcanic,
    dead,
the luminous white of a fisherman's eyes, the roughness of
    rope.

At dusk, the world for a moment contracts.
Even the children are quiet.
Shovels frozen in midair, strands of hair
tangled upwards, defying gravity.
Birds caught still, beaks open,
as if they were about to sing.

When the world starts again, it has slowed down.
The girl is waving to her mother on another dock.
The dog finds another dog and starts to howl.
The sparrow dives into the sea and rises again.
An old man wipes the fog from his glasses with a rag.

Past the dog and the sparrow and the girl,
past the grains of sand circling each other in dance,
past the waves crashing, a human god dying in battle,
past the few notes of a child's singing
audible through waves,
a stillness remains,
a tugboat wailing at its core.

Poem

Light on the mountain
divided by the light of a match.
On the path, a dulled aluminum can tab.
In the sky, lightning's
pre-event flash. As she descends
the cragged rocks,
she avoids the left
snake's hole, the wet
bent twig. What was it
she wanted? An instant
fastened to a thin-beaked bird?

Blue Poem #6

A woman in an "I am here" T-shirt says nothing.

Under ladders, bridges form.

A border erased by waking:

words equal to each other like apples on a white plate.

A cartographer diagraming the contents of his mother's fridge.

(The match you light burns the match.)

How to warn her of the soaked eggs, the curdled milk?

Erased by waking, a border reemerges:

white petals against fingers.

Some words are heavier than others. Try carrying "it."

How to warn them of the weight of "if?"

When we went swimming, his body floated above my out-stretched arms.

How to warn them of the cartographer's joke:

the pool's changed depth:

(Burning the match, we vanish.)

Here, I Say

In my dream Pinocchio is six feet tall.
We are walking on the beach. His wooden palm

pulses in my hand. He says, *Gepetto was wrong,*
lying is the language of trees: a crab shell, sand,

his glass eye gleaming. *If lying is that,*
then what is truth? I want to ask. Instead, I say

I am cataloging my life so I won't forget:
seashells, pebbles, a gull's feather, a swimmer

in a red cap on the horizon. What is the purpose
of *describe?* I long to ask. Pinocchio laughs.

The gulls glide east toward evening.
His tied-on limbs swing awkwardly in the breeze.

Hortence

"It is all summed up in this: to possess sensations and to read nature." —Paul Cézanne

I rid the house of the yarn sphere, the cylinder
vase and the empty wooden box. I stare
at my face in the mirror, let loose
my hair and admire the stringy chaos.
Soon, my husband will be home and I'll sit
for hours in his silent yellow chair.

The light outside is the same as in childhood,
the same as the light on the day
I found the glutinous frog trapped
under the river's rock. Sitting in the living room
while Paul paints, I pretend to like the smell
of turpentine, the burnt umber dizziness,
but I am really ten years old; I poke my finger
into the marsh's shallow border,
yelling because no one I know
is close enough to hear.

The room spins in me. I can hear
the rattle of a neighbor's wagon.
Children down the street play catch
with bean-filled balls, robins sift
through leaves, a creek
passes by, and under it all,
I hear his pink-dipped brush
brush against the canvas's grain.

Nothing Extra

For fifty cents, you enter.
It's darker than you imagined.
There's nothing to see. Just the sound
of crimes on tape, a shot from a rifle,
an old woman screaming, a knife tearing open
a best friend's letter. If you listen
you can recognize the tremble of a third grade
teacher as she spells out
the word 'house,' or the quiet dissolving
of a pacifier in a toddler's jaw.

Let me be clear. This darkness
is not Plato's cave or some pedantic
myth. What is there to prove?
That memory deceives us,
that the thumping of a heart
in an operating theater is indistinguishable
from the beating of first-kissed lips?

Come on. You know a man telling
a joke after a funeral sounds nothing
like a man telling the same joke
after a birth, though both men
have the same waver
of disappointment in their voice.
Similarly, a woman in a movie
waving a scarf sounds nothing
like your own attempt at good-bye,
how when you couldn't find
the Kleenex, you wiped your face
against your kid's stuffed penguin.

You leave the building and it's sunny,
that crass kind of sunny like your mother
saving egg cups for special occasions.

Across the street a photo shop advertises
a yearly sale. They'll take your picture
in someone else's clothes and hair and makeup
for nothing extra. When the stylists are done,
you'll be so beautiful in the wallet-sized prints,
even you won't recognize yourself.

Shtickicsing with the Shtotics

Tashlich

1)

The morning moon is almost invisible
like an image left in a mirror
once the reflected object has pulled away.
Up early, for the first time in weeks, you walk
outside and are surprised:
a dog lurks under a blue car,
a cardinal pecks at a feeder of fat,
its claws clinging to the mesh.

2)

When you were six, a girl shoved
your friend into the lake and you laughed.

When the adult came running
you didn't know what to say.
Silence amplified a buzzing:
cicadas? wires?

Now, what you remember best
are the thick glasses of the adult,
the way her eyes, behind layers of glass,
reflected water,
the way her vowels surrounded you,
erasing all of before.

3)

An afternoon moon hangs where the sun should be.

A rabbi leads his congregation to the river.
A child without shoes is lifted over railroad tracks to water.
A pencil someone dropped flows under a wooden bridge.

Sitting by the edge, you almost recognize
people whispering to each other. You almost hear
the river clear their voices away.

Coney Island Home

—*boardwalk: outside of what remains of Luna and Dreamland Park the day after the fire, May 1911*

If I squint, I can see the lion as he was yesterday, pacing his cage
    as the fire drew near. He was "majestic" in his fear
the headline read. He didn't blink.
    Now, his head points to a money jar covered with stars.
Gold paws stand out against red carpet. Each toe
    larger than my hand. My mother holds me back
from stroking them.
    "He's not alive," I say.
Still, she tugs as if the lion could strike me mute.

Rumor is the lion would have lived. Men whisper it
    in Yiddish as they touch his matted mane.
His hair feels like scales.
    I long to tap his eye to see if he blinks.

"The fire *geshturbin* before it struck his home,"
    a stranger mutters. "We could have sent him
to the Cleveland zoo."
    Children pass through. They poke
the lion with toys. My mother puts her finger
    to her lips—Shh!

By the time the rain ends, the line stretches past
    the boardwalk to shore. A girl sells drinks
and salvaged souvenirs: a brick from Hell,
    a parched sign, ashes in a glass tube.

"It's just as well the trainer shot the lion"
    my mother says as we leave the girl's calls.
"How could our lion have lived away
    from the smell of hot dogs and salt water,
the view of bridges; how could he have
    lived away from home?"

Why the Yellow-Bellied Dragonfly is Not the Only Insect in Maltwood

Every car lolls in its own garage,
the crisp map behind the vinyl steering wheel,
the sunglasses in the empty glove compartment.
Outside, the leaves, immune to wind, crystallize.

Streetlights dim. A girl in her best pink party dress
walks to a birthday party alone, her present decorated
with a stick-on bow. Toilet paper streamers from Halloween
hang damp from the birch. She can hear

a television click off in the house. A man's footsteps
on carpeted stairs. A cat chewing
its food. A broom sweeping a clean floor.
If the moon vanished, dusk would overwhelm her.

Now, she is staring at the huge orange moon. She can feel a
    chill
on her wrists. She can hear a breeze hitting the locked bike's
    metal. Listen:
the buzzing of telephone wires sounds nothing like a field of
    cicadas.

Above

A man pokes a girl's thighs
with a stick as her leg fat droops
between the grates of a mini-
Ferris wheel's seat. Below her shorts,
her leg, like a chicken breast
under plastic, is molded into sections.

When he pulls the lever to *Go,*
she hovers, a story
above crowds and parked cars.
Her cheeks shine
the orange tint of an old TV
Her eyes bulge
like the fat eyes of a happy dog.
"Stop staring," my mother whispers,
pulling my hand
to move me away.
I can not stop.

I love the way she floats
without expression,
the way she hovers,
above crowds and parked cars,
above the balcony
with the rubber plants,
above the grackle
drinking from the roof,
above my mother and me,
both staring—as I tug
at my mother's wet grip,
for her to let me go, and ride.

The Origin of Space

At the lakeside restaurant, the waiter says
I am too big for the high chair
so he brings out an old phone book
for me to sit on. From my perch,
I can see through the window

to the water where an orange ferryboat
of tourists pulls away. The trail of water
behind them forms a sort of animal: a snake

made of water. A fish-shaped banner
strung to the rafters of the boat
swells in the wind. It's so close
I can see the drawn gills on its head.

With each bite of my shrimp,
the boat grows smaller.
First it's the size of the room,

then it's the size of my parents.
When I look up again
the boat has shrunk
to the size of the reflection
in the candle's glass sphere.

The girl I was watching on the deck
has vanished. So has her mother.
Even the giant white
wheel has faded into
the boat's orange body.

I look at my parents. They are still there,
the same size they were.
They don't notice that anything
is happening. They are smiling.
My mom cracks open her lobster claw.
My dad stirs thick milk into his mint tea.

The Orange

My father learned to meditate
in a room behind a curtain.
I could hear him whisper
through the pages of magazines turning.
Zen? I don't remember,
I was five, six maybe. I remember
the oranges on the table, big,
nestled in their gold bird's nest,
five candles lit around them. The reflection
in the mirror magnified them.

A woman in a dark dress
rose, turned her back to us.
She seems almost a shadow
now, rustling in my memory.
She looked down at me
and I felt myself shrink,
the light in the waiting room
flashed white and I glanced down
and saw I was holding one of the big
oranges in my hands, rocking it.
My finger poked below the navel
and I ripped, removing the peel
in one long strip like a snakeskin.

The room let out a scream.
Adults towered over me,
their hair lashing forward and back.
At the end of each strand,
a mouth full of teeth sneered.
I lost track of my father's voice.
The nightingale from the parking lot
slid in through the window,
shedding feathers on clean tables and chairs.
Everyone started to chant.
The carpet turned to pale grass.

My mother returned from the car
with my stuffed penguin and a picture book.
She took the last piece of orange
from my hands and wiped the juice
from my mouth with a towel.
Sorry, she said to the others,
my daughter, you know.
Sorry, she said, *I'm sorry.*

Domestic Comforts

My mother is piling papers
so the housekeeper won't
be startled by the mess.
My father is talking into his miniature
tape recorder, replaying his voice
and pacing the room.
On the bookshelves,
and the table next to the bed,
the books on religion, unread,
whisper to each other.
They squabble in echoes.

If you were to come back the next day
nothing would have changed.
Except this time my mother
might be leafing through the pale
pages of tax return forms,
and my dad might be
yelling into the phone.

By night, they're tired.
They turn the air conditioner on high
and hide themselves in bed
under a puffy down comforter,
too weary now to argue about God.

Yesterday, driving home
from their Jewish humanist group
my father said,
The problem with humanists
is that they don't
use the word God,
and the problem with
rabbis is that they do.

My mother honked the horn
at the oncoming truck and laughed.
She said *The word God is just a metaphor*
for the hand that nudges you into dream
or the transparent feeling you get
when you step into a perfect lake.

My father shrugged, said nothing.
He turned up the radio
and fiddled with the dial
looking for the perfect station,
unable, as always, to find it.

Time's Secret

My father says it to reassure me,
meat from his chicken falling off the bone,
my mother lighting a citronella candle
with a foot-long match. "Imagine
the worst thing that could happen"
he repeats.

Years later, his body
refuses to rest.
Up late visiting,
I watch him hug
a water bottle
and shake.
In the dark,
he memorizes
tapes on sleep
as if mastering
a foreign tongue.

My mother mops the floor with vinegar at dawn.
They are packing to move. Nothing's in the room
but a table, chairs, a roll of bubble wrap.
She says to my father, "Imagine the worst thing
that could happen." He turns off his tape.
The mockingbird by the wire fence imitates a neighbor's drill.

Glow Precedes the Actual Sun

A tree named for some Hindu god gives off persimmon-
scented light. Through the window, my mother
wraps glass, dabs her eyes with a scarf.

She watches as my father, in his jogging suit
and slippers, paces the front lawn,
waiting for sleep.

In my father's last dream, his father returned
to advise him: "Don't shtickics with the shtotics"
my grandfather said. *Of course,*

my father now blurts, rewinding
his meditation tape to the start.
Don't shtickics with the shtotics

Don't stoop to their level. Still, his shoulder's
nerves contract and even as he chants my grandfather's
mantra, his arm, like a marionette's, shakes.

Afterimage

1)

Under old trees, a rabbi hands out xeroxed Kaddishes.
Ink stains his damp hands. He is paid per funeral.

Chanting, he wonders if only the old follow the old prayers.
The rest just watch each other to see who is crying, who is
    looking
at the ground, what kinds of shoes you can wear with black.

Soon, he drives home, passing neighborhoods where Jews
once ran butcher shops and mini-shuls. Now, new immi-
    grants
have settled. Where once he played stickball with the jew-
    eler's son,
there are bodegas with orange signs and the scent of pork
    buns
steaming from dim sum palaces.

2)

Everyone flew to New York on a day's notice: me, from
    Seattle,
my parents from Albuquerque, the body from Boca.

My uncle has covered the mirrors in his living room
but the bathroom mirror, glued to the wall,
remains bare. With the door open,
the mirror reflects the hallway's Hockney print:
a swimming pool after a splash. In the mirror,
I can see the frozen afterimage of a diver—
the reflective white foam at the edge of a wave.

3)

Looking at the photograph we pass around while sitting
   shiva,
everyone sighs at her large eyes and full lips. Each relative
can name a different actress she looks like:
Jane Wyman, Rita Hayworth, Doris Day.

4)

On the road to the graveyard, a woman talks
with a second cousin about publishing.

On the telephone by the rest room, a son whispers
to his lawyer about the estate. The other son counts
relatives and scouts the parking lot for his wife's car.
Finally, one of the sons writes a few lines for the rabbi.

No one says that she was loved or that she loved.

5)

Another photograph is passed around the coffee table:

my grandparents stand on a cruise ship. With cardboard ears
pasted to her head and whiskers drawn on her cheeks,
she is a cat and my grandfather, with nine Life magazines
pasted to his shirt, her nine lives.

Whenever we saw them, and later
when we saw just her,
we were shown this photograph.

Only then, as she reached for it, did she seem happy.

6)

The rabbi lifts the first shovel of dirt and I am nervous
that I will miss my turn, or that I'll trip as I approach the
   grave.

If this were a movie, it would be raining,
gamelan music would be playing.

Now, no one cries.

As I step toward the grave, sun illuminates
the dandruff on my father's new coat.

A cousin brushes the bangs from her eyes.
An uncle bites his white lower lip.

In the distance, I can hear the beep of a car alarm deactivating,
the warm roar of a stranger's engine starting.

Personal Ad

A History of Western Art

1)

The Sumerians coined the term "love" to signify "tie."
The Greeks invented screaming coaches,
the Romans: three-legged races. Before long,
Byzantines were throwing Frisbees across valleys,
while Gothic sculptors lifted weights shaped like wings.

2)

Our history is the "loon" in "hot air balloon."

Leave it at this. Leave as leaves
shroud our fourth meeting.

You could have been more
than the egg in the tempera.

O you, who will always be a you.

3)

By the time the Neoclassicists learned archery,
Romantics had stolen the target.

Realists rode dullness over horse-colored skies.

4)

In every era, we'd meet again,
Impressionists hang-gliding over serial lakes,
Cubists playing squash, Social Realists
piling up sneakers and waterskiing cords
like post-Halloween pumpkins.

Vegetable Cures

Comparing strategies for sleep, we analyze
the varied rest factors of roots:

potatoes bring on balmy womb memories,
carrots signal bit-lip adolescence. I want to ask:

if you were a future philosopher, a medical student
in 1865, cutting open your first cadaver,

would the memory of watching a young woman
change her bicycle's tire haunt you as you removed

the fallen lung or would your head be clear
of past desire, the lung's image implanted in your retina

like the reflection of a camera in an early photographer's
self-portrait? Tonight, talking to you about sleep,

and our lack of it, I think I am that medical student.
I see your talking as a memory of talking.

As I reach for your sleeve, you finish your list
of imagined vegetable cures. *Think of yourself*

as a winter squash, you advise, *picture yourself*
changing color over the earth's frayed cracks.

Love Poem

Something about Nietzsche's pet frog and Lou Andreas-
    Salomé
leaving it on Rilke's doorstep in an empty paint can
sometime before the First World War. When the hysteria
is over (i.e. the chaotic jumping of the drugged-out
frog, the unexpected fainting on the Indian carpet, the
swirling of the sun above) all that exists
is the color green. The Archaic Torso of Apollo,
which at one time plagued me like a secret name
is now a flat stone in the middle of a field.

Does this mean we're in bed again? Mouth open,
half asleep. Damn. I had wanted to go on a boat ride.
Instead, we kiss on my half-made bed till my breast
bone turns red and lumpy, till Rilke has to leave the room
to chill iced tea, till the memory of being seven undressing
the Barbie and Ken dolls with the boys at the next picnic
    table
leaning over my shoulder, pointing and disappointed, finally
    fades away.

Now I'm New and Improved

Once I thought
that kissing was the same
as driving along a highway in
June. Looking up into the other's
eyes was always blue
and obligatory, like a rest stop
on Route 31. What was important
was what one couldn't see: the speed
of wind in red ears, the thoughts of a woman
running by the side of the road,
a silent moaning in an ugly dawn.

Features

1)

We converge under an eyelid,
and he complains he can't see.
Unfortunately, I like it here.
The curator's description
of my ankle turns me on.

2)

The ear confronts the self.

Ear: Did you read today's news?
Self: We cried like infants inside a rattle.
Ear: The music becomes you like a splinter in a tweezer.

When I lowered myself into his words,
my ear was his tongue, the self
was a roller-skating shop clerk hawking
vanishing cream to young nuns.

3)

A woman enters a room carrying two teeth:
one a slab of riotous loss, the other yellow
apology. "I am tired of these derivative choices!"
the window box calls out, "You are like
a stuffed animal, ripped out of its turquoise fur..."

4)

The face of the woman gluing the billboard up
is the same as my face in it.

Damn art with its two-fisted wings.

Give me a room free of meeting—
a nose that doesn't know who I'm not.

The It Before the Here

Enough of this—
give me
those peach pits you placed to dry
next to the window, your joke I overheard
leaning off the balcony
at last week's party.
      I want the traces of you
as well as the you of you,
give me the murmured garble of your voice
on tape, your transparent handprint
on the new glass door.

Why Love Is a Better Antidote to Music Than the Color Blue

Because our eyes are not the dark canvas
we imagine. Because in the world of pure sight
there is no Rothko blue to transport us
like a magic seed—(eat and you will disappear).
Because the leaves of the Moroccan heart plant
peel and open to reveal smaller hidden leaves
and miniature seeds. Seeds denser than
the specks in a loved one's closed eyes.
Because the hand is too clever an organ
to be considered beautiful. Because even as I open
and close my painted mouth to the pale blue sky
I am lying with every breath.

Personal Ad

A couple slumps on a veranda opening flat Cokes.
The ex-girlfriend of the boyfriend and the boyfriend of the ex-
girlfriend play scrabble in mittens. It is that party again,
where I find the personal that reads,
Must be willing to whine and be whined at.

It is not a day for making sandwiches.
A potted shrub blooms a vermilion rash.
The guests are waiting for the spectacle
to denounce its departure.

Must avoid talk about work
when work matters.
Must look potential in-laws in the eye.

A marinated rabbit sizzles on a charcoal grill.
A woman applies lipstick to a Burmese cat.

Must answer telephone messages right away,
I stand on the picnic table to announce,
Must lie and tell me everything is great.

Instruments

Speedometer

My burnt tongue is a new field's white stubble.

Mulched leaf veins cover the porch.

I tried filling the deer-print with water,
but instead the water vanished.

If not, why not?

Grackles space themselves evenly on telephone wires.

Two days after burning, cold water isolates each blister on
    the tongue.

Cars speed by.

As you shift in our bed, I am the bird measuring the distance
    between us.

Thermometer

This is how I remember it. A clock ticked in five tones.
 A cat licked himself in the center of the room.

We were stripping the colors from the walls with our eyes
is how I understood it. We had forgotten the meaning

of chairs. *I am my eyes* I said. A leaf landing
on the cat's back. Your neck sweating like gills.

We had forgotten the mating of hands. *I am I am*
I said, discreetly picking my footprints off the floor.

Letter After Goodbye

What starts as longing turns to loss.
This could be true.

But now, watching trucks creep up the hill,
loss seems a type of vision:
an outline in a camera's lens.

To think: here you were,
a pair of socks rolled under my bed
the vein in my hand you traced one morning
before breakfast. The way you laughed at my laugh.

Only my window has forgotten you,
I'd like to say, noticing the yard scarred with tracks
or the wet fists of leaves covering the old car.

Now, raising the window, I squint to find
the post where you used to lock your bicycle
but get distracted by the iridescent beetles
climbing the peeled ledge.

In a Small Room

The problem with living alone in a single room
is that your parrot remembers sex sounds
and repeats them when you open the shades.
Still, the sun's striped cheeriness
cheers you. Walking toward the mirror,
you see the self you were years ago,
stepping out of a different apartment's bathtub,
shiny like a photographed dolphin between waves.

You might as well set the table for company,
make an inventory of all the words you like
but rarely get to use: quince, estuaries, wreck.
Before long, it will be time to sweep away
some old guest's scattered hair, to speed the arrival
of boxing-nun puppets and windup purple-lipped clowns.

Window as Camouflage

If either of us mentions the other one's name
accidentally in the midst of some argument
about the problems of third-world development
it doesn't mean that the name is a window,
allowing the view of a banana-colored parrot
in an avocado tree. The name could just
as well be a way of hiding, like the girl
who dresses up as "average girl" for Halloween.
Likewise, in the dream where he thinks I am reaching
for him, it is really a bottle of cola, shaken
to resemble a sex act, that pulls me out of bed.

Only those who acknowledge that the blue light
in the make-out closet is calibrated to invoke
paranoia will understand why the TV shows
about shape-shifting aliens never bring
nightmares or why what we accept is no
worse than the quiet of a Thanksgiving
dinner where the turkey carcass
in the middle of the table resembles how he feels
(and me too, though I would never admit it.)

Wrapped Up and Quiet

Discussing the benefits of sanitary devices
with women I barely know, I try to memorize
the order of my boss's niece's toys.
All I had wanted was a perfunctory salutation,
a knock on his vinyl car casing,
a noseprint on glass. But when my old lover
returns, bearing live, sweater-wrapped carp,
I know I'd prefer a stranger's suicide note
to his hands. And when he asks
"Do you want to go swimming
in a suburban lake?" I think someone
must have replaced his brain clock
with a child's pet chicken.
Out the window, construction workers
dangle, stars hover, a hot dog
vender squirts his mustard
in an uninterrupted line. Back in the room,
a woman claims she's mastered
the art of cellophane recycling,
and I feel a buzz of energy
strike us all. What can we accomplish
by recording every second in our veins
and keeping them like this? My friend,
the private stripper, says men
call daily to ask what shoes
she's wearing. Some days in a session,
green-eyed cat watching from the shelf,
the sound of applause from the waiting room TV,
she envies the guy panting on the floor.
She's sure he's found some
quotient of perfection, silent and manifest,
in the buckles of her high-heeled boots.

Prospects in the Present Tense

He said he was missing twelve vital hours
and would need some of mine. This was an opening
of sorts, a break in the onslaught of my days
like the word *possibilities* whispered alone
in a locker room shower. Heck, that chicken
in the chicken suit would rather be a ballet dancer
too! It would trade its skills in divine
mindlessness for a subscription to *Sincerity Today*.

Talk, though, was supposed to provide
an outlet, I'd read and believed the day
we planted seeds wearing 3-D glasses,
the train tracks changing to the brighter
shade of green. It was like the day
he convinced me, in a voice I'd assumed
meant affection, that the girl suspended
by wires over the sleeping audience
hung there through her own sheer will.

In the Midst

Perhaps the ancients knew what they were doing
when they color-coded moods. In my poems,
love's always the same: those smells,
stepping out of a pool, how when I slipped
plastic robots fell from slot machines,
geese threw off their winter scarves.
The poem I started about one man's
feet is now about another man's shoes;
the breakup sobbing has been reduced
to breakup lakes. Still,
the feeling of singular bliss lingers—
that island in the midst of similar islands,
where trumpeters choose to return.

Love Poet Writes About a Field

Buckled tan strands of weeds brush
against my feet. I glimpse a footprint, no,
a shadow in the mud; the rough surface
of a boulder looks like salt deposits in the broken light.

I'll admit it. I am bored by the skinny wildflower
folded near its head, by the one yellow petal left wilting.
From the willow branch an inchworm dangles,
a J shape. Its clear thread vanishes, then glistens.

Once, when I complained about plant poems,
he said "All nature poems are about who you are
in love with, not what you see."

A scrap of computer paper rests buried
in grass, dirt drifting through its bent holes.
White powder flecks a crushed leaf.
Grease on a matted feather shines.